HOMEMADE GRANOLA

HOMEMADE GRANOLA

Delicious Recipes Using Oats & Muesli

Elise Barber

Contents

Introduction

My love affair with granola began with my first taste: peanut butter granola, a combination that remains my favourite to this day. After that first breakfast, I spent the day dreaming of peanut butter granola, and woke up excited for breakfast the next day. At first, I ate only small bowls, convinced that a food this tasty couldn't possibly be good for me. Since learning more about granola, my servings have gotten a whole lot bigger. This particular granola is so beloved by my family that one year I gave my mother the recipe and a big bag of freshly baked peanut butter granola as a Christmas present! While my tastes have since expanded to include many other granola variations (and my Christmas gifts have expanded to include gingerbread granola), these toasty, oaty clusters have remained an irresistible part of my every day. I love the ease of preparing granola and the smell of it baking. I love when I see the empty granola bin in my pantry and immediately start to ponder what granola I should make next. I love feeling decadent by adding chocolate milk to my bowl of granola, or slicing some fresh pears into my spicy gingerbread granola.

For me, it's important that my food is both delicious and healthy. As an elementary music teacher and amateur triathlete, I'm usually eager to get up and out the door, but I don't want to skip breakfast. With its short preparation time and simple baking involved, I find it easy to prepare a double or triple batch of granola on the weekend while planning my week. I then have easy access to my favorite breakfast and snacks through the rest of the week. Since granola keeps and freezes well, it can even be baked in very large quantities and frozen for several weeks. I find that a big bowl of granola keeps me going right through busy mornings.

For my family, granola has since expanded from a breakfast-only food to a staple, any time of day. We find granola particularly useful for hikes and bicycle trips, or long road trips when the last thing we want is another fast food sandwich. Peanut butter granola is a clear crowd favourite, but I also love upgrading a vanilla yogurt with a little vanilla almond granola or tropical granola. The cereal aisle at the supermarket used to be a great temptation for my husband and I, and we could easily find ourselves shoveling handfuls of sugar-laden empty calories into our mouths. However, with a triple batch of banana bread granola at home, I no longer feel the call of those sugar bombs.

I am so excited to share my recipes with you. Whether you're new to granola or just eager to try some new breakfast options, I encourage you to dive right in and make granola a part of your daily routine. It was in the year that my husband Quinn and I spent studying and travelling in Germany that the seeds of this book were really planted. With the help and taste testing skills of Quinn and my dear and supportive friends Bec and Stefan, and many supplies provided by my parents, a hobby that churned out fuel for long biking trips turned into a passion, a whole lot of recipes and eventually this book. I hope that you enjoy making these recipes as much as I do, and more importantly, that you enjoy the granola as much as I do!

A Healthy Start

The health benefits of oats are undeniable. Packed with protein, soluble fiber and important vitamins such as B1 and magnesium, oats are a low-calorie, filling option. Soluble fiber is particularly important for your health. In addition to helping you maintain a healthy digestion, soluble fiber found in oats can help to lower cholesterol. Having a protein-rich breakfast is important to me. Oat-based granola offers plenty of protein, particularly granolas loaded with the extra protein boost of nuts and nut butters.

Many of the other ingredients in granola can also offer lots of health benefits. Fruit and vegetable based granolas allow you to integrate the vitamins from various fresh fruits and vegetables into your breakfast. However, dried fruit, much like store-bought granola, can easily contain preservatives as well as excess fat and sugars. I recommend making your own dried fruit, or reading the labels carefully to make sure you choose products that are as simple and natural as possible.

Nuts and seeds contain healthy fats, proteins, and some, such as flaxseed, hemp hearts, and walnuts, contain necessary omega-3 fatty acids. Depending on the dry mix used, you may be integrating several other grain sources of fiber and vitamins into your granola as well. Granola can easily offer a varied nutritional profile to your day.

While all granola recipes require some sugar and liquid sweeteners, by making your own granola you can carefully track how much sugar you are putting into your diet. The addition of fat is also necessary to the granola, but also necessary to a healthy body and brain. I highly recommend integrating healthy fats into every meal, and not skimping on them in your granola recipes.

Granola can also be a low-calorie option, particularly when it is homemade. Store-bought granolas can be loaded with fat and sugar. By making your own, you can choose a recipe that meets your calorie needs. Despite being a low-calorie meal, the dose of protein and fibre will keep you full right through to lunch, and snacking on granola can help curb cravings. If you're aiming to go as light as possible I recommend trying a fruit-based granola, or one with vegetables like Zucchini bread granola. However, don't be afraid of adding nuts, nut butters and other healthy options to your granola! Balance is key to a healthy diet, and going hungry or cutting out healthy foods simply because they contain calories is not a healthy way to lose weight or maintain a healthy, fit body. Eat what you love in moderation. For me (and I hope for you too!) granola is a great way to begin your healthy, happy day.

Pantry Basics

By stocking your pantry with granola-making staples, you can be well-prepared to always have your new favorite breakfast or snack on hand. While some granola recipes in this book will call for additional ingredients, by having these staple items available you can make life a little easier when preparing breakfasts for the week or whipping up a tasty after-school snack.

GRAINS & CEREALS

The foundation of every granola, the grains used should be rich in fibre and protein. The recipes in this book include a variety of grains, and can easily be mixed and matched as long as volume is maintained.

Oats: The basis of every good granola! Large flaked or rolled oats work best in granola, although quick-cooking oats will also suffice. For gluten-free granola, make sure to buy certified gluten-free oats.

Brown rice cereal: Wholegrain puffed rice helps to add lightness and crispiness to your granola. White puffed rice cereal can also be used. For gluten-free granola, make sure that your brown rice cereal is specified as gluten-free.

SWEETENERS

In addition to contributing to the taste of the granola, sweeteners are also important for helping the granola to clump together, brown beautifully, and have that crunchiness.

Honey: Sweet, sticky, and packed with natural health benefits, honey can be used as the liquid sweetener in many granolas. Honey is more distinct and detectable in granola than maple syrup.

Maple syrup: Mild-tasting and sweet, this Canadian classic often serves as the basis for many of my own granolas. Maple syrup has a thinner texture than honey, and is not as sticky.

Brown sugar: Often my sugar of your choice for the rich molasses flavour, brown sugar can easily be substituted with whatever granulated sugar you have on hand, including white sugar and coconut sugar.

Applesauce: If possible, choose an applesauce with no added sweeteners or sugar, as unsweetened applesauce is sweet enough! Applesauce will add sweetness to your granola, but will also soften the texture. Applesauce has a subtle flavor, and will not overpower in recipes where a stronger flavor is present, such as in peanut butter granola.

SPICES & FLAVORINGS

Vanilla: Seek out a real, good quality vanilla essence (extract) for the best flavor. Avoid imitation extracts or vanilla flavorings. While sometimes more expensive, real vanilla is more flavorful and aromatic, and well worth the investment!

Cinnamon: A key spice to many granolas, cinnamon adds a rich, deep, spicy flavor.

Ginger: With a warm, earthy, zingy flavor, ginger will add depth to recipes in which it is included. I generally use ground ginger, while fresh grated ginger will have a stronger flavor.

Lemon juice: Fresh squeezed lemon juice will have a stronger, brighter flavor than bottled, although either will work in the granola recipes!

OILS, SPREADS & FATS

Vital both to a healthy diet and a delicious granola, fat sources are not only an important source of energy in your breakfast, but also help to coat and crisp up your granola. Different fat sources will add different flavours and textures to your granola, so feel free to try different ones in your granola!

Canola oil: I use canola oil or another neutral-tasting vegetable oil in most of my granola recipes. Versatile and mild, these oils work well in most granolas.

Coconut oil: This nutritious fat adds a distinct coconut flavor to any granola. It should usually be melted before being added to the recipe so it can be distributed evenly through the granola.

Butter or margarine: This fat will make cake or cookie-flavored granolas really taste like the baked good they are imitating!

Nut butters (peanut, almond, hazelnut): I often make my own nut butters, but store-bought ones can be a good shortcut on busy days! Try purchasing natural nut butters, without added sugar or fat.

NUTS, SEEDS & DRIED FRUIT

Choose your favorite dried fruits and nuts to include in your granola. Buy nuts without added salt. Try drying your own fruit, or choose dried fruit with minimal added sugar and fat.

Almonds: I often use slivered almonds in my granola, as I find they distribute well throughout the granola. However, chopped or full-sized almonds will both work as well, according to your preference.

Dried apples: Useful in so many granola recipes, and easily purchased or made, dried apples add sweetness and texture to a large variety of granola recipes in this book.

Flaxseed: I highly recommend adding a tablespoon of ground flaxseed to any recipe for an omega-3 boost. Flaxseeds can be purchased ground, ground in a coffee grinder, or even just added whole!

Dietary Needs

Due to the variety of grains, sweeteners, and fats available, granola can easily be customised to accommodate all types of dietary needs and food allergies. I have included here a list of recommended ingredient substitutions if you have a special dietary need. This guide is by no means comprehensive, and people with food allergies and dietary restrictions must be careful choosing foods they can eat.

GLUTEN-FREE GRANOLA

To create gluten-free granola, use only grains that are certified gluten-free. If you wish to use a dry mix recipe that calls for a wheat-based grain, you may replace it with a gluten-free grain, provided the volume of grain remains the same.

Gluten-free: Oats, puffed rice cereal, buckwheat, oat bran, and quinoa. None of these grains contain gluten, but ensure that the variety you purchase is certified gluten-free.

Contains gluten: Barley flakes, wheat germ, wheat bran, all contain gluten. Replace grains with a gluten-free option such as certified gluten-free corn flakes, oats, or buckwheat.

Risky Foods: Chocolates and other sweets (such as toffee bits) often contain gluten. Make sure that the chocolate used in your granola is certified gluten-free.

LACTOSE-FREE GRANOLA

If you suffer from lactose intolerance, granola is still an easy and healthy option! Many granola recipes in this book are naturally lactose-free, and there are simple changes that can be applied to many of the other recipes to remove all lactose.

Foods containing lactose

Milk: Instead of using regular milk, replacement options include lactose-free milk, almond milk, soy milk, coconut milk, or even apple juice. Any of these can be substituted into the recipe with unnoticeable or minor change to the granola.

Butter: Instead of butter, use a lactose-free margarine or other oil. Good options include coconut oil or canola oil.

Milk/white chocolate: Choose a lactose-free or very dark chocolate instead to minimise lactose consumption. Lactose-free cacao nibs can also replace chocolate chips. Most recipes will still produce a delicious granola even if chocolate chips are simply removed.

Cream cheese: There are some soy-based, lactose-free spreadable or cream cheese options available. If you cannot find these options, it may be best to avoid recipes that call for cream cheese as an ingredient.

Yogurt: There is a wide variety of lactose-free and soy yogurts available that can simply replace the yogurt called for in any recipe. Use your favorite kind, and look for Greek yogurt when possible for the extra dose of protein!

Classic & Basic Granolas

The building blocks of every good granola include a dry mix. To create your granola of your choice, choose a dry mix (either the basic or one of the more complex mixes) and combine with any granola recipe that appeals to you. Flexible and adaptable, these dry mixes will work with any granola recipe in the book. Use this section to customize your granola to suit your own personal tastes.

Basic dry granola mix

MAKES 3 CUPS

This provides a light, crunchy granola using simple ingredients. It is easily made gluten free—just check the cereal packaging to make sure that your oats and rice cereal are made in a gluten-free environment.

---

5 oz (140 g) rolled (porridge)
  oats or large flake oats
1¾ oz (50 g) puffed rice cereal

Combine the ingredients in a large mixing bowl.

Notes: Store in an airtight container at room temperature for up to 3 weeks. You can also freeze the mixture for up to 3 months.

You can use this mix in any of the granola recipe in this book.

Fibre-rich multigrain dry mix

MAKES 3 CUPS

Looking for a way to sneak more fibre into your diet? Try a high-fibre mix disguised as a delicious granola!

---

5 oz (140 g) rolled (porridge)
  oats or large flake oats
1 oz (30 g) bran flake cereal
1¾ oz (50 g) rolled barley flakes
3 tablespoons oat bran
1 tablespoon flaxseed meal
2 tablespoons wheat germ

Combine the ingredients in a large mixing bowl.

Notes: Store in an airtight container for up to 3 weeks.

You can use this mix in any granola recipe. Try Honey pistachio granola, p60 or Rise & shine granola, p33.

Trail mix dry mix

MAKES 3 CUPS

Can't get enough of nuts and seeds? Inspired by an old Barber family granola recipe, you can use this trail-mix granola base in any granola recipe! Watch your granola carefully as it bakes to prevent burning.

5 oz (140 g) rolled (porridge) oats or large flake oats
1½ oz (45 g) pumpkin seeds
¾ oz (20 g) flaked coconut
3½ oz (100 g) nuts of your choice
1½ oz (45 g) sunflower seeds
3½ oz (100 g) dried fruit
1½ oz (40 g) milk chocolate chips (optional)

Combine the oats, pumpkin seeds, coconut, nuts, and sunflower seeds in a large mixing bowl.

After using as a base of a granola recipe of your choice, add dried fruit of your choice and chocolate chips if using.

Notes: Store in an airtight container for up to 3 weeks.

You can use this mix in any granola recipe. Try Chocolate lover's granola, p67 or Banana bread granola, p111.

Quinoa dry mix

MAKES 3 CUPS

5 oz (140 g) rolled or large flake oats
1½ oz (45 g) uncooked quinoa, rinsed
4½ oz (125 g) buckwheat hot cereal mix
2 tablespoons flaxseed meal
2 tablespoons sunflower seeds
¾ oz (20 g) flaked coconut
2 tablespoons chia seeds

If using whole flaxseeds, grind flax in a food processer before using.

Combine the ingredients in a large mixing bowl.

Notes: You can use this mix in any granola recipe. Try Pumpkin spice granola, p110 or Earl grey granola, p106.

Store in an airtight container at room temperature for up to 3 weeks. You can also freeze the mixture for up to 3 months.

Vanilla almond granola

MAKES 3½–4 CUPS

This fragrant granola will make your whole house smell of rich vanilla. Make sure to use a good-quality vanilla for a truly amazing taste! This granola also makes a great base for granola mixes.

1 quantity Basic dry granola mix, p16 or 1 quantity dry granola mix of your choice

3 tablespoons oil

3½ oz (100 g) honey or maple syrup

1½ tablespoons natural vanilla essence (extract)

½ teaspoon almond extract

¼ teaspoon salt

2¼ oz (60 g) chopped or slivered almonds

1½ oz (45 g) dried blueberries or other dried fruit of your choice (optional)

Preheat the oven to 375°F (190°C). Line a baking tray with baking paper.

Combine the oil, honey or maple syrup, vanilla, almond extract and salt in a bowl. Add the dry granola mix to another bowl.

Pour the wet mixture over the dry granola mixture. Use a spatula or wooden spoon to fold together until evenly coated throughout.

Pour the mixture evenly onto the prepared baking tray, taking care that the layer is not too thin around the edges.

Bake in the preheated oven for 15–20 minutes. Remove the tray and spread the chopped or slivered almonds over the granola. Using a spatula or wooden spoon, stir the granola and nuts on the tray gently to combine. Return to the oven and bake for 10–15 minutes, or until the granola is crisp and lightly browned. Check often to prevent burning.

Remove the granola from the oven. Leave to cool for at least 10 minutes. Allow to cool completely before breaking into chunks and storing in an airtight container.

Notes: Store in an airtight container at room temperature for up to 3 weeks. You can also freeze the mixture for up to 3 months.

You can also add 1½ oz (45 g) of dried blueberries or other dried fruit of your choice.

Banana trifle

SERVES 4–8

A lovely layered dessert packed with fruit and crunchy granola, and completely customizable!
This is my husband's go-to dessert.

Pudding:
13 oz (370 g) 1% (skim) milk
**2 tablespoons cornstarch
   (cornflour)**
pinch salt
1 tablespoon sugar
2 ripe bananas, mashed
1 egg yolk
**½ teaspoon natural vanilla
   essence (extract)**

Trifle layers:
1 banana, thinly sliced
**3½ oz (100 g) baked granola
   of your choice, such as
   Vanilla almond, p18 or Salted
   caramel, p75**
**3¼ oz (90 g) whipped cream
   (optional)**

Combine the milk, cornstarch, salt, and sugar in a saucepan over medium–low heat and whisk together until there are no lumps.

Whisk in the egg yolk, then heat until bubbling and thickened enough to coat the back of a spoon. Remove from the heat, and stir in the mashed banana and vanilla. Leave to cool to close to room temperature, stirring occasionally.

Layer the ingredients in a glass or jar. Start with the granola, then add the pudding mixture, banana slices and whipped cream (if using). Repeat.

Serve immediately or refrigerate until ready to serve. Best eaten on the day it is made.

Simple cinnamon granola

MAKES 3 CUPS

Effortlessly tasty and always delicious, this customizable granola is sure to please.

---

1 quantity **Basic dry granola mix, p16** or 1 quantity dry granola mix of your choice
3 tablespoons oil
2 tablespoons honey
1 tablespoon maple syrup
1 tablespoon brown sugar
1 egg white, lightly beaten
½ teaspoon natural vanilla essence (extract)
¼ teaspoon salt
1 teaspoon ground cinnamon

Preheat the oven to 375°F (190°C). Line a baking tray with baking paper.

Combine the oil, honey, maple syrup, brown sugar, egg white, vanilla, salt, and cinnamon in a bowl. Add the dry granola mix to another bowl.

Pour the wet mixture over the dry granola mixture. Use a spatula or wooden spoon to fold together until evenly coated throughout.

Pour the mixture evenly onto the prepared baking tray, taking care that the layer is not too thin around the edges.

Bake in the preheated oven for 25-40 minutes, or until the granola is crisp and lightly browned. Check often to prevent burning.

Remove the granola from the oven. Leave to cool for at least 10 minutes before removing from the tray. Allow to cool completely before breaking into chunks and storing in an airtight container.

Note: Store in an airtight container at room temperature for up to 3 weeks. You can also freeze the mixture for up to 3 months.

Classic fruit & nut granola

MAKES 3½–4 CUPS

This mix-and-match granola can be made to suit any tastes. Choose your favorite nuts and fruit, or just whatever you have on hand!

Simple cinnamon granola, unbaked, p22

2½ oz (75 g) sliced or whole nuts of your choice, such as almonds, macadamias, pistachios, hazelnuts, peanuts, or walnuts.

2½ oz (75 g) roughly chopped dried fruit of your choice, such as apricot, apple, figs, or prunes.

Preheat the oven to 375°F (190°C). Line a baking tray with baking paper.

Prepare the Simple cinnamon granola. Pour the mixture evenly onto the prepared baking tray, taking care that the layer is not too thin around the edges. Bake for 15–20 minutes.

Remove the tray and stir through your nuts of your choice. Return to the oven and bake for a further 10–15 minutes, or until the granola is crisp and lightly browned. Check often to prevent burning.

Remove the granola from the oven. Allow to cool for at least 10 minutes before removing from the tray.

Stir in the dried fruit of your choice. Allow to cool completely before breaking into chunks and storing in an airtight container.

Notes: Store in an airtight container at room temperature for up to 3 weeks. You can also freeze the mixture for up to 3 months.

I like to add peanuts and dried strawberries to my granola, but dried blueberries and almonds are another favorite.

Breakfast parfait

SERVES 1

A large glass layered with yogurt, granola, and fruit is a healthy way to enjoy a protein-rich breakfast.
I love to use vanilla yogurt, peanut butter granola, and sliced strawberries!

5½ oz (150 g) yogurt of your
choice, such as Greek-style,
natural or vanilla

3½ oz (100 g) granola of your
choice (see suggested combos
below)

3¼ oz (90 g) sliced fresh fruit of
your choice

2 tablespoons chia seeds
(optional)

Layer the ingredients in a glass or jar. Start with the granola, then add the yogurt, chia seeds (if using) and the sliced fruit. Repeat.

Serve immediately or refrigerate until ready to serve. Best eaten on the day it is made.

Suggested combinations:

Vanilla almond granola **+** vanilla yogurt **+** blueberries
Peach pie granola **+** Greek-style yogurt **+** fresh peach slices
Honey nut granola **+** coconut-flavoured yogurt **+** sliced banana
Strawberry rhubarb granola **+** natural yogurt **+** shredded coconut
Peanut butter granola **+** vanilla yogurt **+** sliced strawberries
Chai granola **+** vanilla Greek-style yogurt **+** fresh sliced apple

Oatmeal raisin cookie granola

MAKES 3½–4 CUPS

Who wouldn't want to eat cookies for breakfast?

---

1 quantity Basic dry granola
  mix, p16 or 1 quantity dry
  granola mix of your choice
2 tablespoons melted butter
3 tablespoons brown sugar
2 tablespoons honey
1½ teaspoons molasses (not
  blackstrap)
2 tablespoons milk
1 teaspoon vanilla
¼ teaspoon salt
½ teaspoon ground cinnamon
1 oz (25 g) shredded coconut
1¾ oz (50 g) raisins

Preheat the oven to 375°F (190°C). Line a baking tray with baking paper.

Combine the melted butter, sugar, molasses, honey, milk, salt, vanilla, and cinnamon in a bowl. Add the dry granola mix to another bowl.

Pour the wet mixture over the dry granola mixture. Use a spatula or wooden spoon to fold together until evenly coated throughout.

Pour the mixture evenly onto the prepared baking tray, taking care that the layer is not too thin around the edges.

Bake in the preheated oven for 15–20 minutes. Remove the tray, and stir in half of the shredded coconut. Return to the oven and bake for 10–15 minutes, or until the granola is crisp and lightly browned. Check often to prevent burning.

Remove the granola from the oven. Leave to cool for at least 10 minutes before stirring in the raisins and the remaining shredded coconut. Allow to cool completely before breaking into chunks and storing in an airtight container.

Note: Store in an airtight container at room temperature for up to 3 weeks. You can also freeze the mixture for up to 3 months.

Blueberry granola muffins

MAKES 12 MUFFINS

My mother's famous (at least according to my father) blueberry muffin recipe, with my little granola twist!

4½ oz (125 g) all-purpose (plain) flour

2¼ oz (60 g) whole-wheat (wholemeal) flour

½ teaspoon salt

2 teaspoon baking powder

5 oz (140 g) brown sugar

4 tablespoons oil

2½ tablespoons applesauce

1 egg

5 tablespoons milk

3½ oz (100 g) fresh or frozen blueberries

1 teaspoon fresh lemon zest or lemon juice (optional)

⅓ batch baked granola of your choice (I recommend Classic fruit & nut, p23 or Oatmeal raisin cookie, p27)

Granulated raw sugar, for topping (optional)

Preheat the oven to 350°F (180°C). Grease or line a 12-hole muffin tin.

Combine the flour, salt, baking powder and sugar in a bowl.

Combine the oil, applesauce, egg, milk and lemon zest or juice in a small bowl.

Pour the wet ingredients into the dry, and stir the ingredients together until barely combined—do not overmix, or your muffins will be tough! Gently fold in the blueberries and the baked one-third batch granola.

Evenly distribute the batter between the muffin holes. If desired, top with a sprinkling of raw sugar.

Bake for 18–25 minutes, or until a toothpick inserted into the centre comes out clean. Leave to cool in the tin for 5–10 minutes, then remove and leave to cool completely on a wire rack.

Note: Store in an airtight container at room temperature for 3-4 days. You can also freeze the muffins for up to 3 months.

Honey nut granola

MAKES 3½–4 CUPS

If almonds are not to your taste, peanuts would also make a delicious mix-in to this granola!

1 quantity Basic dry granola mix, p16 or 1 quantity dry granola mix of your choice
3 tablespoons oil
4½ oz (125 g) honey
1 tablespoon milk
¼ teaspoon almond essence (extract)
½ teaspoon natural vanilla essence (extract)
¼ teaspoon salt
2¼ oz (60 g) chopped or slivered almonds

Preheat the oven to 375°F (190°C). Line a baking tray with baking paper.

Combine the oil, honey, milk, almond extract, vanilla, and salt in a bowl. Add the dry granola mix to another bowl.

Pour the wet mixture over the dry granola mixture. Use a spatula or wooden spoon to fold together until evenly coated throughout.

Pour the mixture evenly onto the prepared baking tray, taking care that the layer is not too thin around the edges.

Bake in the preheated oven for 15–20 minutes. Remove the tray, and stir in the chopped or slivered almonds. Return to the oven and bake for 10–15 minutes, or until the granola is crisp and lightly browned. Check often to prevent burning.

Remove the granola from the oven. Allow to cool for at least 10 minutes before removing from the pan. Allow to cool completely before breaking into chunks.

Note: Store in an airtight container at room temperature for up to 3 weeks. You can also freeze the mixture for up to 3 months.

Sour cherry granola crisp

SERVES 4–8

A tart but sweet dessert crisp that only gets better with a big scoop of ice cream!

1 lb (450 g) pitted sour cherries
(fresh, frozen, or canned)
3 oz (85 g) sugar
2 tablespoons all-purpose
(plain) flour
½ quantity granola, unbaked,
such as Honey nut, p31 or
Vanilla almond, p18
vanilla ice cream, to serve
(optional)

Preheat the oven to 375°F (190°C). Grease an 8-inch (20 cm) baking dish.

Combine the pitted cherries, sugar, and flour in a large bowl. Pour into the prepared dish.

Prepare the granola, but do not bake. Instead, evenly layer the unbaked granola over the cherry mixture.

Bake for 30–50 minutes, or until the granola is crisp and browned, and fruit is bubbling. Serve immediately, with a scoop of vanilla ice cream if desired.

Note: Store in an airtight container in the refrigerator for up to 1 week.

Rise & shine granola

MAKES 4 CUPS

Tasty granola full of everything that's good for you! A great way to start the morning.

1 quantity Basic dry granola
   mix, p16 or 1 quantity dry
   granola mix of your choice
3 tablespoons coconut oil
1½ oz (45 g) applesauce
¾ oz (20 g) finely grated carrot
2 tablespoons orange juice
1½ teaspoons wheat germ
2 tablespoons brown sugar
2 tablespoons honey or maple
   syrup
½ teaspoon natural vanilla
   essence (extract)
¼ teaspoon salt
1 teaspoon ground cinnamon
3 oz (85 g) mix-ins of your
   choice (feel free to choose as
   many as desired):
— raisins
— walnuts
— shredded coconut
— dried apple

Preheat the oven to 350°F (180°C). Line a baking tray with baking paper.

Combine the coconut oil, applesauce, orange juice, carrot, wheat germ, sugar, sweetener, vanilla, salt, and cinnamon in a large bowl. Add the dry granola mix to another bowl.

Pour the wet mixture over the dry granola mixture. Use a spatula or wooden spoon to fold together until evenly coated throughout.

Pour the mixture evenly onto the prepared baking tray, taking care that the layer is not too thin around the edges.

Bake in the preheated oven for 15–20 minutes. Remove the tray and stir in the nuts, if using. Return to the oven and bake for 10–15 minutes, or until the granola is crisp and lightly browned. Check often to prevent burning.

Remove the granola from the oven. Leave to cool for at least 10 minutes before removing from the tray. Stir in any other mix-ins being used, such as fruit. Allow to cool completely before breaking into chunks and storing in an airtight container.

Note: Store in an airtight container at room temperature for up to 3 weeks. You can also freeze the mixture for up to 3 months.

Chocolate chip cookie granola

MAKES 3½ CUPS

Granola reminiscent of fresh-baked chocolate chip cookies! What could be better?

1 quantity Basic dry granola mix, p16 or 1 quantity dry granola mix of your choice

2 tablespoons melted unsalted butter

3 tablespoons brown sugar

2 tablespoons honey

1½ teaspoons molasses (not blackstrap)

2 tablespoons milk

1 teaspoon natural vanilla essence (extract)

¼ teaspoon salt

½ teaspoon ground cinnamon

2¼ oz (60 g) milk chocolate chips

Preheat the oven to 375°F (190°C). Line a baking tray with baking paper.

Combine the melted butter, sugar, molasses, honey, milk, salt, vanilla, and cinnamon in a bowl. Add the dry granola mix to another bowl.

Pour the wet mixture over the dry granola mixture. Use a spatula or wooden spoon to fold together until evenly coated throughout.

Pour the mixture evenly onto the prepared baking tray, taking care that the layer is not too thin around the edges.

Bake in the preheated oven for 25–35 minutes, or until the granola is crisp and lightly browned. Check often to prevent burning.

Remove the granola from the oven. Leave to cool for at least 10 minutes before stirring in the chocolate chips. Allow to cool completely before breaking into chunks and storing in an airtight container.

Note: Store in an airtight container at room temperature for up to 3 weeks. You can also freeze the mixture for up to 3 months.

Fruit & Nut Granolas

Peach pie granola

MAKES 3½–4 CUPS

Fresh or canned peaches are cooked with honey and cinnamon in this summery granola.

---

1 quantity Basic dry granola
   mix, p16 or 1 quantity dry
   granola mix of your choice
4½ oz (125 g) mashed peach
1½ teaspoons lemon juice
2 tablespoons white sugar
2 tablespoons honey
2 tablespoons butter or
   margarine
½ teaspoon natural vanilla
   essence (extract)
¼ teaspoon salt
¼ teaspoon cinnamon
1½ oz (45 g) chopped or
   slivered almonds
1 oz (30 g) dried peaches

Preheat the oven to 350°F (180°C). Line a baking tray with baking paper.

Add the dry granola mix to a bowl and set aside.

Heat the mashed peach, lemon juice, sugar, honey, butter, vanilla, salt, and cinnamon in a saucepan over medium heat. Bring to a simmer, and cook together uncovered for about 5 minutes.

Pour the wet mixture over the dry mixture. Use a spatula or wooden spoon to fold together until evenly coated throughout.

Pour the mixture evenly onto the prepared baking tray, taking care that the layer is not too thin around the edges.

Bake in the preheated oven for 15–20 minutes. Remove the tray, and stir in chopped or slivered almonds. Return to the oven and bake for 15–20 minutes, or until the granola is crisp and golden. Check often to prevent burning.

Remove the granola from the oven. Leave to cool for 10 minutes, then stir in the dried peaches.

Allow the granola to cool completely before breaking into chunks and storing in an airtight container.

Note: Store in an airtight container at room temperature for up to 3 weeks. You can also freeze the mixture for up to 3 months.

Ginger pear granola

MAKES 3½–4 CUPS

Modeled after my favorite muffin, this granola marries sweet pears with spicy ginger.

1 quantity Basic dry granola mix, p16 or 1 quantity dry granola mix of your choice
4 oz (115 g) mashed pear (1 medium–large pear)
1½ teaspoons lemon juice
2 tablespoons brown sugar
2 tablespoons maple syrup
3 tablespoons oil
½ teaspoon natural vanilla essence (extract)
¼ teaspoon salt
1 teaspoon ginger, or to taste
1 oz (30 g) dried pear or apple
1 oz (30 g) candied ginger

Preheat the oven to 350°F (180°C). Line a baking tray with baking paper.

Add the dry granola mix to a bowl and set aside.

Heat the mashed pear, lemon juice, brown sugar, syrup, oil, vanilla, salt, and ginger in a saucepan over medium heat. Bring to a simmer, and cook together uncovered for about 5 minutes.

Pour the wet mixture over the dry mixture. Use a spatula or wooden spoon to fold together until evenly coated throughout.

Pour the mixture evenly onto the prepared baking tray, taking care that the layer is not too thin around the edges.

Bake in the preheated oven for 25–35 minutes, or until the granola is crisp and golden. Check often to prevent burning.

Remove the granola from the oven. Leave to cool for 10 minutes, then stir in dried fruit.

Allow the granola to cool completely before breaking into chunks and storing in an airtight container.

Note: Store in an airtight container at room temperature for up to 3 weeks. You can also freeze the mixture for up to 3 months.

Strawberry rhubarb granola

MAKES 3½–4 CUPS

Designed after the popular pie, this granola is simultaneously sweet and tart!

1 quantity Basic dry granola
    mix, p16 or 1 quantity dry
    granola mix of your choice
12 oz (340 g) rhubarb, diced
    (approximately 1½–2 large
    stalks)
4 fl oz (120 ml) cold water
2 tablespoons brown sugar
2 tablespoons honey or maple
    syrup
2 tablespoons vegetable or
    coconut oil
½ teaspoon natural vanilla
    essence (extract)
¼ teaspoon salt
¼ teaspoon cinnamon
1 oz (30 g) dried strawberries

Preheat the oven to 350°F (180°C). Line a baking tray with baking paper.

Add the dry granola mix to a bowl and set aside.

Place the diced rhubarb and water in a saucepan, and bring to a boil over medium-high heat. Once the mixture is boiling, reduce the heat to medium-low to maintain a simmer. Stir often to break up the fruit. Simmer for 7–10 minutes with no lid until the fruit is soft and mushy, and there are very few visible lumps.

Combine the cooked rhubarb, sugar, sweetener, oil, vanilla, salt and cinnamon in a bowl.

Pour the wet mixture over the dry mixture. Use a spatula or wooden spoon to fold together until evenly coated throughout.

Pour the mixture evenly onto the prepared baking tray, taking care that the layer is not too thin around the edges.

Bake in the preheated oven for 30-40 minutes, or until the granola is crisp and golden. Check often to prevent burning.

Remove the granola from the oven. Leave to cool for 10 minutes, then stir in the dried strawberries.

Allow the granola to cool completely before breaking into chunks and storing in an airtight container.

Note: Store in an airtight container at room temperature for up to 3 weeks. You can also freeze the mixture for up to 3 months.

Jam or jelly granola

MAKES 3½–4 CUPS

Try any flavor of jam or jelly to offer a huge variety of granolas. I love it made with fresh apricot jam.

---

1 quantity Basic dry granola mix, p16 or 1 quantity dry granola mix of your choice
2 tablespoons oil
1 teaspoon lemon juice
6 tablespoons jam or jelly of your choice
2 tablespoons milk
½ teaspoon natural vanilla essence (extract)
¼ teaspoon salt
pinch of cinnamon (optional)
1 oz (30 g) dried fruit of your choice

Preheat the oven to 325°F (170°C). Line a baking tray with baking paper.

Add the dry granola mix to a bowl and set aside.

Combine the oil, jam/jelly, lemon juice, milk, vanilla, salt, and cinnamon.

Pour the wet mixture over the dry mixture. Use a spatula or wooden spoon to fold together until evenly coated throughout.

Pour the mixture evenly onto the prepared baking tray, taking care that the layer is not too thin around the edges.

Bake in the preheated oven for 30–40 minutes, or until the granola is crisp and golden. Check often to prevent burning.

Remove the granola from the oven. Leave to cool for 10 minutes, then stir in dried fruit.

Allow the granola to cool completely before breaking into chunks and storing in an airtight container.

Note: Store in an airtight container at room temperature for up to 3 weeks. You can also freeze the mixture for up to 3 months.

Lemon blueberry granola

MAKES 3½–4 CUPS

A tangy, light, and refreshing breakfast or snack. The lemon flavor is subtle at first, and then will burst on your tastebuds!

---

1 quantity Basic dry granola mix, p16 or 1 quantity dry granola mix of your choice
2 tablespoons oil
2 tablespoons lemon juice
1 egg white, lightly beaten
2 tablespoons honey or maple syrup
2 tablespoons brown sugar
½ teaspoon lemon extract
¼ teaspoon salt
1 teaspoon lemon zest (optional)
1 oz (30 g) dried blueberries

Preheat the oven to 325°F (170°C). Line a baking tray with baking paper.

Add the dry granola mix to a bowl and set aside.

Combine the oil, lemon juice, lightly beaten egg white, liquid sweetener, brown sugar, lemon extract, salt, and lemon zest in a bowl.

Pour the wet mixture over the dry mixture. Use a spatula or wooden spoon to fold together until evenly coated throughout.

Pour the mixture evenly onto the prepared baking tray, taking care that the layer is not too thin around the edges.

Bake in the preheated oven for 30–40 minutes, or until the granola is crisp. Broil (grill) on high for a further 2-3 minutes for extra-crunchy granola. Check often to prevent burning.

Remove the granola from the oven. Leave to cool for at least 10 minutes, then stir in the dried blueberries. Allow to cool completely before breaking into chunks and storing in an airtight container.

Note: Store in an airtight container at room temperature for up to 3 weeks. You can also freeze the mixture for up to 3 months.

Tropical granola

MAKES 3½–4 CUPS

Eating this granola brings back memories of sipping tropical drinks on the beach!

1 quantity Basic dry granola
  mix, p16 or 1 quantity dry
  granola mix of your choice
3 tablespoons coconut oil
3 oz (85 g) crushed pineapple
2 tablespoons honey
2 tablespoons brown sugar
½ teaspoon natural vanilla
  essence (extract)
¼ teaspoon salt
1 teaspoon rum or rum extract
  (optional)
1½ oz (45 g) dried pineapple
1 oz (30 g) shredded coconut
1½ oz (45 g) chopped
  macadamia nuts

Preheat the oven to 350°F (180°C). Line a baking tray with baking paper.

Add the dry granola mix to a bowl and set aside.

Combine the coconut oil, crushed pineapple, honey, brown sugar, vanilla, salt, and rum extract.

Pour the wet mixture over the dry mixture. Use a spatula or wooden spoon to fold together until evenly coated throughout.

Pour the mixture evenly onto the prepared baking tray, taking care that the layer is not too thin around the edges.

Bake in the preheated oven for 25-35 minutes, or until the granola is crisp and lightly browned. Check often to prevent burning.

Remove the granola from the oven. Leave to cool for at least 10 minutes, then stir in chopped nuts, dried pineapple, and coconut. Allow to cool completely before breaking into chunks and storing in an airtight container.

Note: Store in an airtight container at room temperature for up to 3 weeks. You can also freeze the mixture for up to 3 weeks.

Banana granola yogurt bites

SERVES 1–2

A tasty frozen treat that works great as a breakfast on the go, or a healthy snack.

1 banana, cut into thirds
2¼ oz (60 g) yogurt of your choice
1¾ oz (50 g) granola of your choice

Place the yogurt and the granola in two separate shallow bowls.

Dip each banana piece into the yogurt, coating thoroughly. Coat each banana piece in the granola. Freeze for at least 1 hour.

Notes: If desired, you can insert popsicle sticks into the end of each banana segment for easier handling.

Once frozen, the bananas can be placed in a sealed bag in the freezer for 1 week.

I like to use Vanilla almond granola, p18, with mixed berry yogurt.

Apple strudel granola

MAKES 3½–4 CUPS

The popular flavors of Austrian apple strudel, or simply of apple pie!

1 quantity Basic dry granola mix, p16 or 1 quantity dry granola mix of your choice
2 tablespoons melted butter
4½ oz (125 g) applesauce
2 tablespoons honey or maple syrup
2 tablespoons brown sugar
½ teaspoon natural vanilla essence (extract)
¼ teaspoon salt
2 teaspoons apple pie spice
1½ teaspoons cinnamon
¼ teaspoon ginger
pinch of allspice
1 oz (30 g) dried apple pieces
1 oz (30 g) raisins
1½ oz (45 g) chopped walnuts or pecans

Preheat the oven to 350°F (180°C). Line a baking tray with baking paper.

Add the dry granola mix to a bowl and set aside.

Combine the melted butter, applesauce, liquid sweetener, sugar, vanilla, salt, and spices in a bowl.

Pour the wet mixture over the dry mixture. Use a spatula or wooden spoon to fold together until evenly coated throughout.

Pour the mixture evenly onto the prepared baking tray, taking care that the layer is not too thin around the edges.

Bake in the preheated oven for 30-40 minutes, or until the granola is crisp and lightly browned. Check often to prevent burning.

Remove the granola from the oven. Leave to cool for at least 10 minutes, then stir in chopped nuts, dried apples, and raisins. Allow to cool completely before breaking into chunks and storing in an airtight container.

Note: Store in an airtight container at room temperature for up to 3 weeks. You can also freeze the mixture for up to 3 weeks.

Key lime granola

MAKES 3½–4 CUPS

Fresh, tangy key lime flavor makes this granola reminiscent of one of my favorite pies!

1 quantity Basic dry granola mix, p16 or 1 quantity dry granola mix of your choice
2 tablespoons oil
2 tablespoons lime juice
1 egg white, lightly beaten
2 tablespoons honey or maple syrup
2 tablespoons brown sugar
½ teaspoon lime essence (extract)
¼ teaspoon salt
1 teaspoon lime zest

Preheat the oven to 325°F (170°C). Line a baking tray with baking paper.

Add the dry granola mix to a bowl and set aside.

Combine the oil, lemon juice, lightly beaten egg white, liquid sweetener, brown sugar, lemon extract, salt, and lemon zest in a bowl.

Pour the wet mixture over the dry mixture. Use a spatula or wooden spoon to fold together until evenly coated throughout.

Pour the mixture evenly onto the prepared baking tray, taking care that the layer is not too thin around the edges.

Bake in the preheated oven for 30-40 minutes, or until the granola is crisp. Broil (grill) on high for a further 2-3 minutes for extra-crunchy granola. Check often to prevent burning.

Remove the granola from the oven. Leave to cool for at least 10 minutes, then stir in dried cranberries. Allow to cool completely before breaking into chunks and storing in an airtight container.

Note: Store in an airtight container at room temperature for up to 3 weeks. You can also freeze the mixture for up to 3 weeks.

Peanut butter granola

MAKES 3½–4 CUPS

My personal long-time favorite granola, reminiscent of fresh peanut butter cookies!

1 quantity Basic dry granola
mix, p16 or 1 quantity dry
granola mix of your choice

2¼ oz (65 g) unsweetened
applesauce

3¼ oz/ (95 g) natural peanut
butter

1 tablespoon oil

1½ tablespoons brown sugar

1½ tablespoons honey or maple
syrup

½ teaspoon natural vanilla
essence (extract)

¼ teaspoon salt

1¾ oz (50 g) peanuts

Preheat the oven to 325°F (170°C). Line a baking tray with baking paper.

Add the dry granola mix to a bowl and set aside.

Combine the applesauce, peanut butter, oil, sugar, syrup, vanilla, and salt in a bowl.

Pour the wet mixture over the oats and rice cereal. Use a spatula or wooden spoon to fold together until evenly coated throughout.

Pour the mixture evenly onto the prepared baking tray, taking care that the layer is not too thin around the edges.

Bake in the preheated oven for 15 minutes, then remove the baking tray from the oven and sprinkle the peanuts onto the granola.

Continue baking for a further 10-20 minutes, or until the granola is crisp and dark golden. Broil (grill) on high for a further 2-3 minutes for extra-crunchy granola.

Remove the granola from the oven. Leave to cool for at least 10 minutes before removing from the tray, and allow to cool completely before breaking it into chunks and storing in an airtight container.

Note: Store in an airtight container at room temperature for up to 3 weeks. You can also freeze the mixture for up to 3 months.

Peanut butter & jelly granola

MAKES 3½–4 CUPS

This granola will take you back to your childhood lunches! Sweet and salty all at the same time.

1 quantity Basic dry granola mix, p16 or 1 quantity dry granola mix of your choice
2¼ oz (65 g) unsweetened applesauce
3¼ oz (95 g) natural peanut butter
3 tablespoons jam or jelly of your choice (try raspberry, strawberry, or grape. I like to use strawberry!)
1 tablespoon oil
½ teaspoon natural vanilla essence (extract)
¼ teaspoon salt
1¾ oz (50 g) peanuts
1 oz (30 g) dried berries such as strawberries or raspberries

Preheat the oven to 325°F (170°C). Line a baking tray with baking paper.

Add the dry granola mix to a bowl and set aside.

Combine the applesauce, peanut butter, oil, sugar, syrup, vanilla, and salt in a bowl until well mixed.

Pour the wet mixture over the oats and rice cereal. Use a spatula or wooden spoon to fold together until evenly coated throughout.

Pour the mixture evenly onto the prepared baking tray, taking care that the layer is not too thin around the edges.

Bake in the preheated oven for 15 minutes, then remove the baking tray from the oven and sprinkle the peanuts onto the granola.

Continue baking for a further 10-20 minutes, or until the granola is crisp and dark golden. Broil on high for a further 2-3 minutes for extra-crunchy granola.

Remove the granola from the oven. Leave to cool for at least 10 minutes before removing from the tray, and allow to cool completely before breaking it into chunks and storing in an airtight container.

Note: Store in an airtight container at room temperature for up to 3 weeks. You can also freeze the mixture for up to 3 months.

White chocolate macadamia nut granola

MAKES 3½–4 CUPS

Sweet and full of buttery macadamia nuts, this granola will keep you coming back for more!

1 quantity Basic dry granola
  mix, p16 or 1 quantity dry
  granola mix of your choice
2 tablespoons melted unsalted
  butter
3 tablespoons brown sugar
1½ teaspoons molasses (not
  blackstrap)
2 tablespoons honey
2 tablespoons milk
¼ teaspoon salt
1 teaspoon natural vanilla
  essence (extract)
½ teaspoon ground cinnamon
2¼ oz (60 g) white chocolate
  chips
1¾ oz (50 g) chopped
  macadamia nuts

Preheat the oven to 375°F (190°C). Line a baking tray with baking paper.

Add the dry granola mix to a bowl and set aside.

Combine the melted butter, sugar, molasses, honey, milk, salt, vanilla, and cinnamon in a bowl.

Pour the wet mixture over the dry granola mixture. Use a spatula or wooden spoon to fold together until evenly coated throughout.

Pour the mixture evenly onto the prepared baking tray, taking care that the layer is not too thin around the edges.

Bake in the preheated oven for 25–35 minutes, or until the granola is crisp and lightly browned. Check often to prevent burning.

Remove the granola from the oven. Leave to cool for at least 10 minutes before stirring in the chocolate chips and macadamia nuts. Allow to cool completely before breaking into chunks and storing in an airtight container.

Note: Store in an airtight container at room temperature for up to 3 weeks. You can also freeze the mixture for up to 3 months.

Chocolate peanut butter granola

MAKES 3½–4 CUPS

Rich taste without being too sweet, this granola is great for breakfast or dessert.
I like to eat it with chocolate milk!

1 quantity Basic dry granola
mix, p16 or 1 quantity dry
granola mix of your choice
2¼ oz (65 g) unsweetened
applesauce
3¼ oz (95 g) natural peanut
butter
1 tablespoon oil
1½ tablespoons brown sugar
2 tablespoons cocoa powder
1½ tablespoons honey or maple
syrup
½ teaspoon natural vanilla
essence (extract)
¼ teaspoon salt
1¾ oz (50 g) peanuts
1½ oz (45 g) chocolate chips

Preheat the oven to 325°F (170°C). Line a baking tray with
baking paper.

Add the dry granola mix to a bowl and set aside.

Combine the applesauce, peanut butter, oil, sugar, cocoa powder,
syrup, vanilla, and salt in a bowl.

Pour the wet mixture over the oats and rice cereal. Use a spatula or
wooden spoon to fold together until evenly coated throughout.

Pour the mixture evenly onto the prepared baking tray, taking care
that the layer is not too thin around the edges.

Bake in the preheated oven for 15 minutes, then remove the baking
tray from the oven and sprinkle the peanuts onto the granola.

Continue baking for a further 10-20 minutes, or until the granola
is crisp and dark golden. Broil on high for a further 2-3 minutes for
extra-crunchy granola.

Remove the granola from the oven. Leave to cool for at least
10 minutes before removing from the tray. Add choc chips. and
allow to cool completely before breaking it into chunks and storing
in an airtight container.

Note: Store in an airtight container at room temperature for up to
3 weeks. You can also freeze the mixture for up to 3 months.

Chocolate hazelnut granola

MAKES 3½–4 CUPS

Chocolate and hazelnuts for breakfast are a delicious and protein-packed option!

1 quantity **Basic dry granola mix, p16 or 1 quantity dry granola mix of your choice**

2½ oz (70 g) **chocolate hazelnut spread**

2¼ oz (65 g) **unsweetened applesauce**

1 tablespoon **oil or milk**

½ teaspoon **natural vanilla essence (extract)**

¼ teaspoon **salt**

2¼ oz (60 g) **chopped hazelnuts**

Preheat the oven to 325°F (170°C). Line a baking tray with baking paper.

Add the dry granola mix to a bowl and set aside.

Combine the chocolate hazelnut spread, applesauce, oil or milk, vanilla, and salt in a bowl.

Pour the wet mixture over the dry mixture. Use a spatula or wooden spoon to fold together until evenly coated throughout.

Pour the mixture evenly onto the prepared baking tray, taking care that the layer is not too thin around the edges.

Bake in the preheated oven for 15 minutes, then remove the baking tray from the oven and sprinkle the chopped hazelnuts onto the granola.

Continue baking for a further 10-20 minutes, or until the granola is crisp and browned.

Remove the granola from the oven. Leave to cool for at least 10 minutes. Allow to cool completely before breaking into chunks and storing in an airtight container.

Note: Store in an airtight container at room temperature for up to 3 weeks. You can also freeze the mixture for up to 3 months.

No-bake granola energy balls

MAKES 12

Sweetened with dates and flavored with peanut butter, these tasty snacks
will keep you going through the whole day!

3 oz (85 g) dates (soak for
  10 minutes in water prior
  to using)
2 tablespoons natural peanut
  butter
1 teaspoon cocoa powder
1 teaspoon honey
1¾ oz (50 g) granola of your
  choice, such as Chocolate
  peanut butter, p56 or Honey
  nut, p31

Add the dry granola mix to a bowl and set aside.

Place the soaked dates into a blender or food processor, and blend
until quite smooth.

Add the peanut butter, cocoa powder, and honey to the food
processor, and process until all ingredients are blended. If too solid
to blend, add up to 2 teaspoons of water.

Add the dry granola mixture and pulse to break up and mix in
the granola.

Scoop out the mixture and, using your hands, form into balls. Serve
at room temperature.

Note: Store in an airtight container in the refrigerator for up to
3 weeks. You can also freeze the energy balls for up to 3 months.

Honey pistachio granola

MAKES 3½–4 CUPS

Fragrant and reminiscent of baklava, this subtly nutty granola makes a great snack.

1 quantity Basic dry granola mix, p16 or 1 quantity dry granola mix of your choice

2 tablespoons oil
1 oz (30 g) raw pistachios, ground
3½ oz (105 g) honey
2½ tablespoons milk
1½ teaspoons lemon juice
½ teaspoon natural vanilla essence (extract)
¼ teaspoon salt
½ teaspoon cinnamon
¼ teaspoon ground cloves
¼ teaspoon ground cardamom (optional)

1¾ oz (50 g) shelled pistachios, chopped or whole

Preheat the oven to 325°F (170°C). Line a baking tray with baking paper.

Add the dry granola mix to a bowl and set aside.

Combine the oil, ground pistachios, honey, milk, lemon juice, vanilla, salt, and spices in a bowl.

Pour the wet mixture over the dry granola mix. Use a spatula or wooden spoon to fold together until evenly coated throughout.

Pour the mixture evenly onto the prepared baking tray, taking care that the layer is not too thin around the edges.

Bake in the preheated oven for 25 minutes, then remove the baking tray from the oven and sprinkle the pistachios onto the granola.

Continue baking for a further 5-15 minutes, or until the granola is crisp and dark golden.

Remove the granola from the oven. Leave to cool for at least 10 minutes before removing from the tray, and allow to cool completely before breaking it into chunks and storing in an airtight container.

Note: Store in an airtight container at room temperature for up to 3 weeks. You can also freeze the granola for up to 3 months.

Almond butter granola

MAKES 3½–4 CUPS

All the nutrition of almonds and oats—packed into one hearty and delicious bowl of granola!

1 quantity Basic dry granola mix, p16 or 1 quantity dry granola mix of your choice

2¼ oz (65 g) unsweetened applesauce

3¼ oz (95 g) almond butter

1 tablespoon oil

1½ tablespoons brown sugar

1½ tablespoons honey or maple syrup

½ teaspoon natural vanilla essence (extract)

¼ teaspoon salt

1½ oz (45 g) slivered almonds

Preheat the oven to 325°F (170°C). Line a baking tray with baking paper.

Add the dry granola mix to a bowl and set aside.

Combine the applesauce, almond butter, oil, sugar, syrup, vanilla, and salt in a bowl.

Pour the wet mixture over the oats and rice cereal. Use a spatula or wooden spoon to fold together until evenly coated throughout.

Pour the mixture evenly onto the prepared baking tray, taking care that the layer is not too thin around the edges.

Bake in the preheated oven for 15 minutes, then remove the baking tray from the oven and sprinkle the almonds onto the granola.

Continue baking for a further 10-20 minutes, or until the granola is crisp and dark golden. Broil (grill) on high for a further 2-3 minutes for extra-crunchy granola.

Remove the granola from the oven. Leave to cool for at least 10 minutes before removing from the tray, and allow to cool completely before breaking it into chunks and storing in an airtight container.

Note: Store in an airtight container at room temperature for up to 3 weeks. You can also freeze the mixture for up to 3 months.

Maple pecan granola

MAKES 3½–4 CUPS

This sticky sweet and nutty granola comes from my Canadian kitchen to yours!

1 quantity Basic dry granola mix, p16 or 1 quantity dry granola mix of your choice
2 tablespoons oil
3 oz (85 g) maple syrup
2 teaspoons brown sugar
2 teaspoons light molasses
1 egg white, lightly beaten
½ teaspoon natural vanilla essence (extract)
¼ teaspoon salt
1½ oz (40 g) chopped pecans

Preheat the oven to 325°F (170°C). Line a baking tray with baking paper.

Add the dry granola mix to a bowl and set aside.

Combine the oil, maple syrup, brown sugar, egg white, molasses, salt, vanilla, and pecans in a bowl.

Pour the wet mixture over the dry mixture. Use a spatula or wooden spoon to fold together until evenly coated throughout.

Pour the mixture evenly onto the prepared baking tray, taking care that the layer is not too thin around the edges.

Bake in the preheated oven for 30-35 minutes, or until crisp and lightly browned. Check often to prevent burning.

Remove the granola from the oven. Leave to cool for at least 10 minutes before removing from the tray. Allow to cool completely before breaking into chunks and storing in an airtight container.

Note: Store in an airtight container at room temperature for up to 3 weeks. You can also freeze the mixture for up to 3 months.

Chocolate & Caramel Granolas

Chocolate lover's granola

MAKES 3½–4 CUPS

Rich and chocolatey, a great treat to satisfy the cravings of any chocolate lover!

1 quantity Basic dry granola mix, p16 or 1 quantity dry granola mix of your choice

3 tablespoons oil

3 tablespoons honey or maple syrup (for extra-rich granola, use chocolate syrup)

1 tablespoon brown sugar

3 tablespoons cocoa powder

½ teaspoon natural vanilla essence (extract)

¼ teaspoon salt

1½ oz (45 g) white chocolate chips

1½ oz (45 g) dark chocolate chips

1½ oz (45 g) chopped roasted hazelnuts or cacao nibs (optional)

Preheat the oven to 325°F (170°C). Line a baking tray with baking paper.

Add the dry granola mix to a bowl and set aside.

Combine the oil, liquid sweetener, brown sugar, cocoa powder, salt, and vanilla in a bowl.

Pour the wet mixture over the dry mixture. Use a spatula or wooden spoon to fold together until evenly coated throughout.

Pour the mixture evenly onto the prepared baking tray, taking care that the layer is not too thin around the edges.

Bake in the preheated oven for 30-35 minutes, or until the granola is crisp and browned. Check often to prevent burning.

Remove the granola from the oven. Leave to cool for at least 10 minutes before removing from the tray. Once granola is almost cool, stir in white and dark chocolate chips. If using optional mix-ins, stir in once granola is completely cooled. Allow to cool completely before breaking into chunks and storing in an airtight container.

Note: Store in an airtight container at room temperature for up to 3 weeks. You can also freeze the mixture for up to 3 months.

VARIATION
Aztec chocolate granola

Add ½ teaspoon cinnamon and 1 teaspoon chili powder to wet mixture. Remove mix-ins if desired.

Chocolate chip granola cookies

MAKES 24–30

This classic cookie has a satisfying crunch. I make batches of these for friends and family.

7½ oz (210 g) all-purpose (plain) flour
½ teaspoon baking powder
½ teaspoon baking soda
5½ oz (150 g) butter or margarine
7 oz (200 g) brown sugar
1 egg
1 teaspoon vanilla
2½ oz (75 g) granola of your choice, such as Chocolate lover's, p67 or Salted caramel, p75
3¼ oz (90 g) chocolate chips

Preheat the oven to 350°F (180°C). Line a baking tray with baking paper.

Using electric beaters, beat the butter and sugar in a large bowl until fluffy. Add the egg and vanilla, and beat until combined.

Stir in the flour, baking powder, and baking soda until combined. Stir in the chocolate chips and granola.

Drop heaped teaspoons onto the prepared baking tray. Bake for 10 minutes, or until lightly browned.

Remove from the oven. Leave to cool for at least 10 minutes. Allow to cool completely before storing in an airtight container.

Note: Store in an airtight container at room temperature for up to 1 week.

German chocolate granola

MAKES 3½–4 CUPS

Sweet coconut and chocolate make up this decadent granola modeled after German chocolate cake.

---

1 quantity Basic dry granola mix, p16 or 1 quantity dry granola mix of your choice

2 tablespoons brown or white sugar

1 tablespoon water

¾ oz (20 g) shredded coconut

2 tablespoons coconut oil

2 tablespoons cocoa powder

2 tablespoons milk

2 tablespoons honey or maple syrup

2 tablespoons brown sugar

½ teaspoon natural vanilla essence (extract)

¼ teaspoon salt

Preheat the oven to 325°F (170°C). Line a baking tray with baking paper.

Add the dry granola mix to a bowl and set aside.

Heat 2 tablespoons sugar with 1 tablespoon water in a small saucepan over medium heat. Bring to the boil, then add the shredded coconut. Continue to boil until the coconut is candied, and sugar is crystallized to the coconut, and no longer liquid. Remove from the heat immediately and spread out on baking paper to cool.

Combine the coconut oil, cocoa powder, milk, liquid sweetener, sugar, vanilla, and salt in a bowl.

Pour the wet mixture over the dry mixture. Use a spatula or wooden spoon to fold together until evenly coated throughout.

Pour the mixture evenly onto the prepared baking tray, taking care that the layer is not too thin around the edges.

Bake in the preheated oven for 30-35 minutes, or until the granola is crisp and browned. Check often to prevent burning.

Remove the granola from the oven. Leave to cool for at least 10 minutes before removing from the tray. Stir in candied coconut. Allow to cool completely before breaking into chunks and storing in an airtight container.

Note: Store in an airtight container at room temperature for up to 3 weeks. You can also freeze the mixture for up to 3 months.

71

Chocolate coconut granola muffins

MAKES 12 MUFFINS

Not too sweet, these granola-studded muffins make a great breakfast or midday snack.

6½ oz (185 g) all-purpose (plain) flour or spelt flour

5½ oz (150 g) brown or coconut sugar

2¼ oz (60 g) cocoa powder

1 oz (30 g) shredded coconut

2 teaspoons baking powder

¾ teaspoon salt

1 egg

9 fl oz (250 ml) milk

4½ oz (125 g) plain Greek yogurt or coconut Greek yogurt

1¾ oz (50 g) coconut oil, melted, or oil

2½ oz (75 g) frozen cherries, any excess liquid drained (optional)

3¼ oz (90 g) chocolate chips (optional)

1¾ oz (50 g) granola of your choice, such as German chocolate, p71 or Chocolate lover's, p67

Preheat the oven to 375°F (190°C). Lightly grease a 12-cup muffin pan.

Combine the flour, sugar, salt, baking powder, cocoa powder, and shredded coconut in a bowl.

Combine the oil, egg, milk, yogurt in a separate bowl.

Slowly pour the wet ingredients into the dry, and stir the ingredients together until barely combined—do not over-mix, or your muffins will be tough!

Gently fold in the cherries and chocolate chips, if using.

Evenly distribute the batter between the muffin cups. Crush the granola, then sprinkle over the top of each muffin. Gently press the granola into the batter.

Bake for 18-25 minutes, or until a toothpick inserted into the center comes out clean.

Note: Store in an airtight container at room temperature for up to 1 week.

Chocolate mint granola

MAKES 3½–4 CUPS

Rejoice, lovers of mint and chocolate! Now these flavors can make up a healthy breakfast.
Also delicious over ice cream!

1 quantity Basic dry granola
   mix, p16 or 1 quantity dry
   granola mix of your choice
3 tablespoons oil
1 teaspoon mint essence
   (extract)
3 tablespoons honey or maple
   syrup (for extra-rich granola,
   use chocolate syrup)
1 tablespoon brown sugar
3 tablespoons cocoa powder
½ teaspoon natural vanilla
   essence (extract)
¼ teaspoon salt
3¼ oz (90 g) dark chocolate
   chips

Preheat the oven to 325°F (170°C) Line a baking tray with
baking paper.

Add the dry granola mix to a bowl and set aside.

Combine the oil, mint essence, honey or maple syrup, brown sugar,
cocoa powder, salt, and vanilla in a bowl.

Pour the wet mixture over the dry mixture. Use a spatula or
wooden spoon to fold together until evenly coated throughout.

Pour the mixture evenly onto the prepared baking tray, taking care
that the layer is not too thin around the edges.

Bake in the preheated oven for 30-35 minutes, or until the granola
is crisp and browned. Check often to prevent burning.

Remove the granola from the oven. Leave to cool for at least
10 minutes before removing from the tray.

Once granola is almost cool, stir in the dark chocolate chips. Allow
to cool completely before breaking into chunks and storing in an
airtight container.

Note: Store in an airtight container at room temperature for up to
3 weeks. You can also freeze the mixture for up to 3 months.

Salted caramel granola

MAKES 3½–4 CUPS

Sweet, salty, crisp, and absolutely delicious!

---

1 quantity Basic dry granola mix, p16 or 1 quantity dry granola mix of your choice
6 oz (170 g) caramel sauce
½ teaspoon natural vanilla essence (extract)
½ teaspoon salt, or more to taste
1 tablespoon milk
1½ oz (45 g) toffee bits/caramel chips

Preheat the oven to 325°F (170°C). Line a baking tray with baking paper.

Add the dry granola mix to a bowl and set aside.

Combine the caramel sauce, vanilla, salt, and milk, if needed, in a bowl.

Pour the wet mixture over the dry mixture. Use a spatula or wooden spoon to fold together until evenly coated throughout.

Pour the mixture evenly onto the prepared baking tray, taking care that the layer is not too thin around the edges.

Bake in the preheated oven for 30-35 minutes, until the granola is crisp and lightly browned. Check often to prevent burning.

Remove the granola from the oven. Leave to cool for at least 10 minutes before removing from the tray.

Stir in the toffee bits/caramel chips. Allow to cool completely before breaking into chunks and storing in an airtight container.

Note: Store in an airtight container at room temperature for up to 3 weeks. You can also freeze the mixture for up to 3 months.

Caramel granola cake

SERVES 8

Caramel and crunchy granola baked right into a not-too-sweet butter cake makes a delightful dessert or afternoon snack! Feel free to substitute your favorite cake recipe.

Cake
3½ oz (100 g) unsalted butter, softened
4¾ oz (135 g) granulated sugar
1 teaspoon natural vanilla essence (extract)
2 eggs
6½ oz (185 g) all-purpose (plain) flour
2 teaspoons baking powder
¾ teaspoon salt
5¾ oz (165 g) milk

2¼ oz (65 g) granola of your choice, I recommend Salted caramel, p75 or Honey nut, p31
1 quantity Caramel sauce, p118

Preheat the oven to 350°F (180°C). Grease a 9-inch (23 cm) round cake tin and line with baking paper.

Using electric beaters, beat the butter and sugar in a large bowl until smooth, fluffy, and free of lumps. Add the vanilla and eggs, and beat well.

Combine the flour, baking powder, and salt. Add in thirds to the wet ingredients, alternating with the milk, and mixing between additions.

Pour the cake batter into the prepared tin. Sprinkle the granola over the top. Then take half of the prepared caramel sauce and drizzle over the granola-covered batter.

Bake for 25-35 minutes, or until a toothpick inserted into the center comes out clean.

Serve with reserved caramel sauce, ice cream, or fruit preserves.

Note: Store in an airtight container at room temperature for up to 1 week.

Caramel peanut butter granola

MAKES 3½–4 CUPS

Tastes just like peanut brittle! Amazing over ice cream. Don't expect to stop after just one bite!

---

1 quantity Basic dry granola mix, p16 or 1 quantity dry granola mix of your choice
6 oz (170 g) caramel sauce
1½ oz (45 g) peanut butter
1 tablespoons milk
½ teaspoon natural vanilla essence (extract)
¼ teaspoon salt
1¾ oz (50 g) peanuts
1½ oz (45 g) toffee bits/caramel chips

Preheat the oven to 325°F (170°C). Line a baking tray with baking paper.

Add the dry granola mix to a bowl and set aside.

Combine the caramel sauce, peanut butter, milk, vanilla, and salt.

Pour the wet mixture over the dry mixture. Use a spatula or wooden spoon to fold together until evenly coated throughout.

Pour the mixture evenly onto the prepared baking tray, taking care that the layer is not too thin around the edges.

Bake in the preheated oven for 15–20 minutes. Remove the tray, and add the peanuts. Return to the oven and bake for 10–15 minutes, or until the granola is crisp and lightly browned. Check often to prevent burning.

Remove the granola from the oven. Leave to cool for at least 10 minutes before removing from the tray.

Stir in the toffee bits/caramel chips. Allow to cool completely before breaking into chunks and storing in an airtight container.

Note: Store in an airtight container at room temperature for up to 3 weeks. You can also freeze the mixture for up to 3 months.

Chocolate raspberry granola

MAKES 3½–4 CUPS

1 quantity Basic dry granola
mix, p16 or 1 quantity dry
granola mix of your choice
3 tablespoons oil
3¾ oz (110 g) fresh or frozen
raspberries, mashed
2 tablespoons honey or maple
syrup
2 tablespoons brown sugar
2 tablespoons cocoa powder
½ teaspoon natural vanilla
essence (extract)
¼ teaspoon salt
1½ oz (45 g) chocolate chips
1½ oz (45 g) dried raspberries

Preheat the oven to 350°F (180°C). Line a baking tray with
baking paper.

Add the dry granola mix to a bowl and set aside.

Place the mashed raspberries, oil, liquid sweetener, sugar, cocoa
powder, vanilla, and salt in a saucepan over medium heat. Bring to a
simmer, and cook, uncovered, for about 1 minute.

Pour the wet mixture over the dry mixture. Use a spatula or
wooden spoon to fold together until evenly coated throughout.

Pour the mixture evenly onto the prepared baking tray, taking care
that the layer is not too thin around the edges.

Bake in the preheated oven for 25-35 minutes, or until the granola
is crisp and browned. Check often to prevent burning.

Remove the granola from the oven. Leave to cool for at least
10 minutes before removing from the tray. Stir in the chocolate
chips and dried raspberries. Allow to cool completely before
breaking into chunks and storing in an airtight container.

Note: Store in an airtight container at room temperature for up to
3 weeks. You can also freeze the mixture for up to 3 months.

VARIATION
Chocolate strawberry granola
Replace the mashed raspberries with mashed strawberries, and the
dried raspberries with dried strawberries.

Caramel apple granola

MAKES 3½–4 CUPS

You don't need to go to a carnival for the caramel apples when you have this granola!

---

1 quantity Basic dry granola mix, p16 or 1 quantity dry granola mix of your choice

6 oz (170 g) caramel sauce

2 tablespoons applesauce

½ teaspoon natural vanilla essence (extract)

¼ teaspoon salt

1 tablespoon of milk (optional)

1½ oz (45 g) dried apple pieces

1½ oz (45 g) toffee bits/caramel chips

Preheat the oven to 325°F (170°C). Line a baking tray with baking paper.

Add the dry granola mix to a bowl and set aside.

Combine caramel sauce, applesauce, vanilla, salt, and milk if needed.

Pour the wet mixture over the dry mixture. Use a spatula or wooden spoon to fold together until evenly coated throughout.

Pour the mixture evenly onto the prepared baking tray, taking care that the layer is not too thin around the edges.

Bake in the preheated oven for 15–20 minutes. Remove the tray, and add the peanuts. Return to the oven and bake for 10–15 minutes, or until the granola is crisp and lightly browned. Check often to prevent burning.

Remove the granola from the oven. Leave to cool for at least 10 minutes before removing from the tray.

Stir in the dried apples and toffee bits/caramel chips. Allow to cool completely before breaking into chunks and storing in an airtight container.

Note: Store in an airtight container at room temperature for up to 3 weeks. You can also freeze the mixture for up to 3 months.

Chocolate caramel pecan granola

MAKES 3½–4 CUPS

These flavors blend together to create a fantastic dessert-like granola!

1 quantity Basic dry granola mix, p16 or 1 quantity dry granola mix of your choice
6 oz (170 g) caramel sauce
1½ teaspoons oil
1½ tablespoons cocoa powder
½ teaspoon natural vanilla essence (extract)
¼ teaspoon salt
1 tablespoon of milk (optional)
1½ oz (40 g) chopped pecans
1½ oz (45 g) chocolate chips (optional)
1½ oz (45 g) toffee bits/caramel chips (optional)

Preheat the oven to 325°F (170°C). Line a baking tray with baking paper.

Add the dry granola mix to a bowl and set aside.

Combine the caramel sauce, oil, cocoa powder, vanilla, salt, pecans, and milk, if needed

Pour the wet mixture over the dry mixture. Use a spatula or wooden spoon to fold together until evenly coated throughout.

Pour the mixture evenly onto the prepared baking tray, taking care that the layer is not too thin around the edges.

Bake in the preheated oven for 30-35 minutes, or until the granola is crisp and browned. Check often to prevent burning.

Remove the granola from the oven. Leave to cool for at least 10 minutes before removing from the tray.

Stir in the chocolate chips and toffee bits/caramel chips, if using. Allow to cool completely before breaking into chunks and storing in an airtight container.

Note: Store in an airtight container at room temperature for up to 3 weeks. You can also freeze the mixture for up to 3 months.

Special Treats

S'mores granola

MAKES 3½–4 CUPS

The popular campfire snack, in granola form!

---

1 quantity Basic dry granola
    mix, p16 or 1 quantity dry
    granola mix of your choice
2 tablespoons oil
1¾ oz (50 g) graham cracker
    crumbs
3 oz (85 g) honey
1 tablespoon brown sugar
1 tablespoon wheat bran
2 tablespoons milk
½ teaspoon natural vanilla
    essence (extract)
¼ teaspoon salt
1½ oz (45 g) chocolate chips
½ oz (15 g) mini marshmallows

Preheat the oven to 325°F (170°C). Line a baking tray with baking paper.

Add the dry granola mix to a bowl and set aside.

Combine the oil, graham cracker crumbs, honey, milk, wheat bran, brown sugar, salt, and vanilla.

Pour the wet mixture over the dry mixture. Use a spatula or wooden spoon to fold together until evenly coated throughout.

Pour the mixture evenly onto the prepared baking tray, taking care that the layer is not too thin around the edges.

Bake in the preheated oven for 30 minutes, or until the granola is crisp and lightly browned. Check often to prevent burning.

Remove the granola from the oven. Leave to cool for at least 10 minutes before removing from the tray.

When granola is almost cool, stir in the chocolate chips. Allow to cool completely, then break up granola into chunks. Stir in the mini marshmallows.

Note: Store in an airtight container at room temperature for up to 3 weeks. You can also freeze the mixture for up to 3 months.

Chocolate cheesecake granola

MAKES 3½–4 CUPS

Creamy, cheesy, and full of chocolate flavor, what more could you want from a bowl of granola?

1 quantity Basic dry granola
   mix, p16 or 1 quantity dry
   granola mix of your choice
1 tablespoon melted butter
1½ tablespoons cocoa powder
3¼ oz (90 g) cream cheese
   (full-fat or light, not fat-free)
1¾ oz (50 g) white sugar
1 teaspoon lemon juice
1 egg white, lightly beaten
1 teaspoon wheat bran
½ teaspoon natural vanilla
   essence (extract)
¼ teaspoon salt

Preheat the oven to 325°F (170°C) Line a baking tray with baking paper.

Add the dry granola mix to a bowl and set aside.

Combine melted butter, cocoa powder, cream cheese, sugar, lemon juice, lightly beaten egg white, wheat bran, vanilla, and salt.

Pour the wet mixture over the dry mixture. Use a spatula or wooden spoon to fold together until evenly coated throughout.

Pour the mixture evenly onto the prepared baking tray, taking care that the layer is not too thin around the edges.

Bake in the preheated oven for 15–20 minutes. Remove from oven, add almonds, and put back in for 10–15 more minutes, until lightly browned. Check often to prevent burning.

Remove the granola from the oven. Leave to cool for at least 10 minutes before removing from the tray. Allow to cool completely. Break granola into chunks, and store in an airtight container.

Note: Store in an airtight container at room temperature for up to 3 weeks. You can also freeze the mixture for up to 3 weeks.

Black forest granola

MAKES 3½–4 CUPS

Designed after the popular German treat, Schwarzwälder Kirschtorte,
often referred to as Black Forest Cake.

---

1 quantity Basic dry granola mix, p16 or 1 quantity dry granola mix of your choice

3 tablespoons melted butter

2¼ oz (60 g) cherry jam or mashed cherries cooked with 1 tablespoon sweetener of your choice

2 tablespoons cocoa powder

1½ teaspoon rum extract/kirschwasser/alcohol of your choice

½ teaspoon natural vanilla essence (extract)

¼ teaspoon salt

1½ oz (40 g) dried cherries

Preheat the oven to 325°F (170°C). Line a baking tray with baking paper.

Add the dry granola mix to a bowl and set aside.

Combine the melted butter, cherry jam/cooked cherries, cocoa powder, alcohol/rum extract, vanilla, and salt.

Pour the wet mixture over the dry mixture. Use a spatula or wooden spoon to fold together until evenly coated throughout.

Pour the mixture evenly onto the prepared baking tray, taking care that the layer is not too thin around the edges.

Bake in the preheated oven for 30-35 minutes, or until the granola is crisp and browned. Check often to prevent burning.

Remove the granola from the oven. Leave to cool for at least 10 minutes before removing from the tray. Stir in the dried cherries. Allow to cool completely before breaking into chunks and storing in an airtight container.

Note: Store in an airtight container at room temperature for up to 3 weeks. You can also freeze the mixture for up to 3 months.

Cookies & cream granola

MAKES 3½–4 CUPS

Use boxed cookie crumbs, or make your own from your favorite chocolate biscuit!

1 quantity Basic dry granola
mix, p16 or 1 quantity dry
granola mix of your choice

2 tablespoons oil

1¾ oz (50 g) chocolate cookie
crumbs

1 tablespoon brown sugar

3 tablespoons honey or maple
syrup

2 tablespoons milk

½ teaspoon natural vanilla
essence (extract)

¼ teaspoon salt

1½ oz (45 g) white chocolate
chips

¾ oz (20 g) chocolate cookie
pieces (optional)

Preheat the oven to 325°F (170°C). Line a baking tray with baking paper.

Add the dry granola mix to a bowl and set aside.

Combine the oil, chocolate cookie crumbs, liquid sweetener, brown sugar, milk, vanilla, and salt until well mixed.

Pour the wet mixture over the dry mixture. Use a spatula or wooden spoon to fold together until evenly coated throughout. Stir in chocolate cookie pieces if desired.

Pour the mixture evenly onto the prepared baking tray, taking care that the layer is not too thin around the edges.

Bake in the preheated oven for 30 minutes, or until the granola is crisp and lightly browned. Check often to prevent burning.

Remove the granola from the oven. Leave to cool for at least 10 minutes before removing from the tray. Once the granola is almost cool, stir in the white chocolate chips. Allow to cool completely before breaking into chunks and storing in an airtight container.

Note: Store in an airtight container at room temperature for up to 3 weeks. You can also freeze the mixture for up to 3 months.

Marshmallow granola slice

An oaty twist on a classic treat, these easy and customizable bars have a snappy crunch and a flavorful sweetness.

---

3 tablespoons butter or margarine

7 oz (200 g) marshmallows (preferably mini marshmallows)

1 lb 5 oz (610 g) granola of your choice (I recommend Carrot cake, p108 or Cookies & cream, p93)

Grease an 8 x 8 inch (20 x 20 cm) square baking tin.

In a large saucepan, melt the butter or margarine over low heat. Add the marshmallows to the pot, and stir until completely melted.

Turn off the heat, and use a buttered spatula to quickly stir in the granola of your choice until coated. Firmly press the mixture into the greased dish until it evenly fills the pan.

Leave to cool before slicing into squares and serving.

Note: Store in an airtight container at room temperature for up to 1 week.

Cherry cheesecake granola

MAKES 3½–4 CUPS

Creamy, rich granola. Crumble it up and use it as a cheesecake crust or top it with milk for breakfast!

1 quantity Basic dry granola
    mix, p16 or 1 quantity dry
    granola mix of your choice
1 tablespoon melted butter
3¼ oz (90 g) cream cheese
    (full-fat or light, not fat-free)
1¾ oz (50 g) white sugar
1 teaspoon lemon juice
1 egg white, lightly beaten
1 teaspoon wheat bran
¼ teaspoon almond extract
    (optional)
½ teaspoon natural vanilla
    essence (extract)
¼ teaspoon salt
1½ oz (40 g) cup dried cherries
1½ oz (45 g) chopped or
    slivered almonds

Preheat the oven to 325°F (170°C). Line a baking tray with baking paper.

Add the dry granola mix to a bowl and set aside.

Combine the melted butter, cream cheese, sugar, lemon juice, lightly beaten egg white, wheat bran, almond extract, vanilla, and salt.

Pour the wet mixture over the dry mixture. Use a spatula or wooden spoon to fold together until evenly coated throughout.

Pour the mixture evenly onto the prepared baking tray, taking care that the layer is not too thin around the edges.

Bake in the preheated oven for 15–20 minutes. Remove from the oven, add the almonds, and bake for a further 10–15 minutes, or until lightly browned. Check often to prevent burning.

Remove the granola from the oven. Leave to cool for at least 10 minutes before removing from the tray. Allow to cool completely, then stir in the dried cherries. Break the granola into chunks, and store in an airtight container.

Note: Store in an airtight container at room temperature for up to 3 weeks. You can also freeze the mixture for up to 3 weeks.

VARIATION
Graham-crust cheesecake granola
Prepare both Strawberry cheesecake granola, p99, and S'mores granola, p88, without the chocolate or marshmallows. Mix the granolas together after baking.

Granola-crust cheesecake

MAKES 3½–4 CUPS

A classic-tasting cheesecake with a delicious oaty crust.

Crust:
5½ oz (150 g) granola of your
  choice, such as Gingersnap,
  p101 or S'mores, p88
  (without the marshmallow
  and chocolate)
3 tablespoons unsalted butter
  or margarine, melted

Cheesecake:
1 lb 2 oz (500 g) cream cheese,
  softened
4¾ oz (135 g) Greek yogurt,
  plain or flavor of your choice
3½ oz (100 g) white sugar
2 teaspoons vanilla essence
  (extract)
2 teaspoons lemon juice
2 eggs

Preheat the oven to 325°F (170°C). Lightly grease an 8-inch (20 cm) springform tin.

To make the crust, place the granola into a food processor, and blend until coarsely ground (about 30 seconds to 1 minute).

Combine with the melted butter, and then press firmly into the base of the prepared baking tin. Bake for 5 minutes.

To make the cheesecake, combine all of the ingredients using electric beaters until smooth. Pour the mixture into the granola crust-lined tin.

Bake for 40–60 minutes, or until the center is only slightly jiggly. Remove from the oven. The cheesecake will finish setting once out of the oven. Leave to cool before serving.

Note: Store in an airtight container in the refrigerator for up to 1 week.

Strawberry cheesecake granola

MAKES 3½–4 CUPS

This rich and flavorful granola, full of both calcium and fibre, will keep you full all morning!

1 quantity Basic dry granola mix, p16 or 1 quantity dry granola mix of your choice
1 tablespoon melted butter
3¼ oz (90 g) cream cheese (full-fat or light, not fat-free)
1¾ oz (50 g) white sugar
1 teaspoon lemon juice
1 egg white, lightly beaten
1 teaspoon wheat bran
½ teaspoon natural vanilla essence (extract)
¼ teaspoon salt
1½ oz (40 g) cup dried strawberries
1½ oz (45 g) chopped or slivered almonds

Preheat the oven to 325°F (170°C) Line a baking tray with baking paper.

Add the dry granola mix to a bowl and set aside.

Combine the melted butter, cream cheese, sugar, lemon juice, lightly beaten egg white, wheat bran, vanilla, and salt.

Pour the wet mixture over the dry mixture. Use a spatula or wooden spoon to fold together until evenly coated throughout.

Pour the mixture evenly onto the prepared baking tray, taking care that the layer is not too thin around the edges.

Bake in the preheated oven for 15–20 minutes. Remove from oven, add almonds, and put back in for 10–15 more minutes, until lightly browned. Check often to prevent burning.

Remove the granola from the oven. Leave to cool for at least 10 minutes before removing from the tray. Allow to cool completely, then stir in the dried strawberries and slivered almonds. Break granola into chunks, and store in an airtight container.

Note: Store in an airtight container at room temperature for up to 3 weeks. You can also freeze the mixture for up to 3 weeks.

Gingersnap granola

MAKES 3½–4 CUPS

A classic cookie as granola. Add even more ginger if desired!

1 quantity Basic dry granola mix, p16 or 1 quantity dry granola mix of your choice
2 tablespoons melted butter
1 tablespoon molasses (not blackstrap)
2 tablespoons brown sugar
2 tablespoons maple syrup
1 tablespoon milk
½ teaspoon natural vanilla essence (extract)
¼ teaspoon salt
2 teaspoon ground ginger, or to taste
1 teaspoon ground cinnamon
¼ teaspoon nutmeg
¼ teaspoon cloves
1½ oz (40 g) candied ginger (optional)

Preheat the oven to 325°F (170°C). Line a baking tray with baking paper.

Add the dry granola mix to a bowl and set aside.

Combine the melted butter, molasses, sugar, maple syrup, milk, vanilla, salt, and spices.

Pour the wet mixture over the dry mixture. Use a spatula or wooden spoon to fold together until evenly coated throughout.

Pour the mixture evenly onto the prepared baking tray, taking care that the layer is not too thin around the edges.

Bake in the preheated oven for 30-35 minutes, or until the granola is crisp and browned. Check often to prevent burning.

Remove the granola from the oven. Leave to cool for at least 10 minutes before removing from the tray.

Stir in the candied ginger, if using. Allow to cool completely before breaking into chunks and storing in an airtight container.

Note: Store in an airtight container at room temperature for up to 3 weeks. You can also freeze the mixture for up to 3 months.

Mocha granola

MAKES 3½–4 CUPS

Coffee lovers rejoice! Get your caffeine kick from your breakfast cereal.

---

1 quantity Basic dry granola mix, p16 or 1 quantity dry granola mix of your choice
2 tablespoons oil
3 oz (85 g) strong coffee
2½ oz (75 g) brown sugar
½ tablespoons cocoa powder
½ teaspoon natural vanilla essence (extract)
¼ teaspoon salt
1½ oz (45 g) chocolate chips (optional)
chocolate-covered coffee beans, chopped (optional)

Preheat the oven to 325°F (170°C). Line a baking tray with baking paper.

Add the dry granola mix to a bowl and set aside.

Combine the oil, coffee, brown sugar, cocoa powder, salt, and vanilla.

Pour the wet mixture over the dry mixture. Use a spatula or wooden spoon to fold together until evenly coated throughout.

Pour the mixture evenly onto the prepared baking tray, taking care that the layer is not too thin around the edges.

Bake in the preheated oven for 30-35 minutes, or until the granola is crisp and browned. Check often to prevent burning.

Remove the granola from the oven. Leave to cool for at least 10 minutes before removing from the tray.

Once the granola is almost cool, stir in the chocolate chips and chocolate-covered coffee beans, if using. Allow to cool completely before breaking into chunks and storing in an airtight container.

Note: Store in an airtight container at room temperature for up to 3 weeks. You can also freeze the mixture for up to 3 months.

Apple pear breakfast crisp

SERVES 4–6

A favorite breakfast for fall, this lightly sweet fruit crumble is easy to prep at night and bake in the morning!

---

2 medium–large apples
2–3 ripe pears
1 tablespoon lemon juice
2 tablespoon brown sugar
½ teaspoon cinnamon
½ teaspoon ginger
½ recipe quantity of granola, unbaked, such as Gingersnap, p101
vanilla ice cream, to serve (optional)

Preheat the oven to 375°F (190°C). Grease a 9-inch (23 cm) baking dish.

Peel the apples and chop into small pieces. Chop the pears, and toss in a bowl with the apples. Add the lemon juice immediately, and stir to coat the fruit.

Add the sugar and spices, toss until evenly coated, and place the mixture in the baking dish.

Prepare the granola, but do not bake. Evenly layer the unbaked granola over the chopped fruit mixture.

Bake for 30–50 minutes, or until the granola is crisp and browned, and the fruit is bubbly. Serve immediately, with vanilla ice cream, if you like.

Earl grey granola

MAKES 3½–4 CUPS

Subtly flavored, this granola will be a favorite among true tea lovers.

1 quantity **Basic dry granola mix, p16 or 1 quantity dry granola mix of your choice**
2 tablespoons oil
3 oz (85 g) strong earl grey tea
3 tablespoons honey
1 tablespoon brown sugar
½ teaspoon natural vanilla essence (extract)
¼ teaspoon salt
1 tablespoon lemon juice
pinch of cinnamon (optional)
1¾ oz (50 g) cup nuts of your choice (optional)

Preheat the oven to 325°F (170°C) Line a baking tray with baking paper.

Add the dry granola mix to a bowl and set aside.

Combine the oil, tea, honey, brown sugar, lemon juice, salt, vanilla, and cinnamon.

Pour the wet mixture over the dry mixture. Use a spatula or wooden spoon to fold together until evenly coated throughout.

Pour the mixture evenly onto the prepared baking tray, taking care that the layer is not too thin around the edges.

Bake in the preheated oven for 30-35 minutes, or until the granola is crisp and lightly browned. Stir nuts in halfway through, if using. Check often to prevent burning.

Remove the granola from the oven. Leave to cool for at least 10 minutes before removing from the tray. Allow to cool completely before breaking into chunks and storing in an airtight container.

Note: Store in an airtight container at room temperature for up to 3 weeks. You can also freeze the mixture for up to 3 weeks.

Chai granola

MAKES 3½–4 CUPS

Spicy chai tea makes a flavorful granola.

1 quantity Basic dry granola
    mix, p16 or 1 quantity dry
    granola mix of your choice
2 tablespoons oil
3 oz (85 g) strong chai tea
3 tablespoons honey
½ teaspoon natural vanilla
    essence (extract)
¼ teaspoon salt
½ teaspoon cinnamon
¼ teaspoon ginger
pinch of allspice
pinch of cloves
pinch of cardamom

Preheat the oven to 325°F (170°C). Line a baking tray with baking paper.

Add the dry granola mix to a bowl and set aside.

Combine the oil, chai tea, honey, vanilla, salt, and spices.

Pour the wet mixture over the dry mixture. Use a spatula or wooden spoon to fold together until evenly coated throughout.

Pour the mixture evenly onto the prepared baking tray, taking care that the layer is not too thin around the edges.

Bake in the preheated oven for 30-35 minutes, or until the granola is crisp and lightly browned. Stir halfway through baking time and check often to prevent burning.

Remove the granola from the oven. Leave to cool for at least 10 minutes before removing from the tray. Allow to cool completely before breaking into chunks and storing in an airtight container.

Note: Store in an airtight container at room temperature for up to 3 weeks. You can also freeze the mixture for up to 3 weeks.

Carrot cake granola

MAKES 3½–4 CUPS

Sweet and creamy, fill this granola with your favorite carrot cake mix-ins!

1 quantity Basic dry granola mix, p16 or 1 quantity dry granola mix of your choice

2 tablespoons melted butter

2½ oz (75 g) grated carrot

3¼ oz (90 g) light or full-fat cream cheese (not fat-free)

3 tablespoons brown sugar

2 tablespoons honey or maple syrup

½ teaspoon natural vanilla essence (extract)

¼ teaspoon salt

1½ teaspoon cinnamon

¼ teaspoon nutmeg

3¼ oz (90 g) mix-ins of your choice:

chopped walnuts

raisins

candied ginger

orange zest

shredded coconut

dried pineapple

Preheat the oven to 325°F (170°C). Line a baking tray with baking paper.

Add the dry granola mix to a bowl and set aside.

Combine the melted butter, shredded carrot, cream cheese, sugar, liquid sweetener, vanilla, salt, and spices.

Pour the wet mixture over the dry mixture. Use a spatula or wooden spoon to fold together until evenly coated throughout.

Pour the mixture evenly onto the prepared baking tray, taking care that the layer is not too thin around the edges.

Bake in the preheated oven for 30-35 minutes, or until the granola is crisp and browned. Check often to prevent burning.

Remove the granola from the oven. Leave to cool for at least 10 minutes before removing from the tray. Once the granola is cool, stir in mix-ins of your choice. Allow to cool completely before breaking into chunks and storing in an airtight container.

Note: Store in an airtight container at room temperature for up to 3 weeks. You can also freeze the mixture for up to 3 weeks.

Pumpkin spice granola

MAKES 3½–4 CUPS

Homey fall flavors make this hearty granola a treat in any season!
Goes especially well with your morning pumpkin spice latte.

1 quantity Basic dry granola mix, p16 or 1 quantity dry granola mix of your choice
3 tablespoons oil
3¼ oz (90 g) canned or pureed pumpkin
3 tablespoons maple syrup
1 tablespoon brown sugar
1 egg white, lightly beaten
¼ teaspoon molasses (not blackstrap)
½ teaspoon natural vanilla essence (extract)
2 teaspoons pumpkin pie spice, or to taste
½ teaspoon cinnamon
¼ teaspoon salt
1 oz (30 g) pumpkin seeds (optional)

Preheat the oven to 350°F (180°C). Line a baking tray with baking paper.

Add the dry granola mix to a bowl and set aside.

Combine the oil, pumpkin, maple syrup, brown sugar, lightly beaten egg white, molasses, vanilla, pumpkin pie spice, cinnamon, and salt.

Pour the wet mixture over the dry mixture. Use a spatula or wooden spoon to fold together until evenly coated throughout.

Pour the mixture evenly onto the prepared baking tray, taking care that the layer is not too thin around the edges.

Bake in the preheated oven for 30-40 minutes, or until the granola is crisp. Check often to prevent burning.

Remove the granola from the oven. Leave to cool for at least 10 minutes, then stir in the pumpkin seeds. Allow to cool completely before breaking into chunks and storing in an airtight container.

Note: Store in an airtight container at room temperature for up to 3 weeks. You can also freeze the mixture for up to 3 weeks.

Banana bread granola

MAKES 3½–4 CUPS

A healthier and protein-rich version of the popular loaf cake.
Add in whatever you like in your banana bread!

1 quantity Basic dry granola mix, p16 or 1 quantity dry granola mix of your choice
2 tablespoons melted butter
1½ bananas, mashed
2 tablespoons honey or maple syrup
2 tablespoons brown sugar
½ teaspoon natural vanilla essence (extract)
¼ teaspoon salt
½ teaspoon cinnamon
1½ oz (45 g) dried banana chips
1½ oz (45 g) chopped walnuts or pecans
1½ oz (45 g) chocolate chips (optional)
1½ oz (45 g) peanut butter chips (optional)

Preheat the oven to 350°F (180°C). Line a baking tray with baking paper.

Add the dry granola mix to a bowl and set aside.

Combine the melted butter, mashed banana, liquid sweetener, sugar, vanilla, salt, and cinnamon.

Pour the wet mixture over the dry mixture. Use a spatula or wooden spoon to fold together until evenly coated throughout.

Pour the mixture evenly onto the prepared baking tray, taking care that the layer is not too thin around the edges.

Bake in the preheated oven for 30-40 minutes, or until the granola is crisp and lightly browned. Check often to prevent burning.

Remove the granola from the oven. Leave to cool for at least 10 minutes, then stir in banana chips and chopped nuts and any optional mix-ins, if using. Allow to cool completely before breaking into chunks and storing in an airtight container.

Note: Store in an airtight container at room temperature for up to 3 weeks. You can also freeze the mixture for up to 3 weeks.

Zucchini bread granola

MAKES 3½–4 CUPS

Packed with nutrition, this granola is a tasty way to integrate vegetables into your breakfast!

1 quantity Basic dry granola mix, p16 or 1 quantity dry granola mix of your choice
2 tablespoons melted butter
2½ oz (75 g) finely grated or puréed zucchini, lightly squeezed to remove some of the moisture
2 tablespoons cocoa powder
2 tablespoons brown sugar
2 tablespoons honey or maple syrup
½ teaspoon natural vanilla essence (extract)
¼ teaspoon salt
1 teaspoon cinnamon
1½ oz (45 g) chocolate chips
1½ oz (45 g) chopped walnuts or pecans

Preheat the oven to 325°F (170°C). Line a baking tray with baking paper.

Add the dry granola mix to a bowl and set aside.

Combine the melted butter, zucchini, cocoa powder, sugar, liquid sweetener, vanilla, salt, and cinnamon.

Pour the wet mixture over the dry mixture. Use a spatula or wooden spoon to fold together until evenly coated throughout.

Pour the mixture evenly onto the prepared baking tray, taking care that the layer is not too thin around the edges.

Bake in the preheated oven for 15–20 minutes, then remove from the oven and add the chopped nuts. Bake for a further 10–15 minutes, or until the granola is crisp and browned. Check often to prevent burning.

Remove the granola from the oven. Leave to cool for at least 10 minutes before removing from the tray.

When the granola is almost cool, add the chocolate chips. Allow to cool completely before breaking into chunks and storing in an airtight container.

Note: Store in an airtight container at room temperature for up to 3 weeks. You can also freeze the mixture for up to 3 weeks.

Nut Butters, Sauces & Mix-ins

Peanut butter

MAKES 1¼ CUPS

Unsweetened, this peanut butter tastes only of peanuts and salt, and
is perfect for a rich, peanutty granola.

**10½ oz (300 g) raw, unsalted
peanuts with skins**
½ teaspoon salt, or to taste

Preheat the oven to 350°F (180°C). Line a baking tray with baking
paper.

Spread the peanuts, with skins on, evenly over the baking tray. Roast
in the preheated oven for 10 minutes. The oil in the nuts should
come to the surface, making the peanuts shiny.

Allow the peanuts to cool for 5 minutes. Process the peanuts, with
skins, in a food processor for approximately 3 minutes, or until the
peanut butter is smooth and soft. Add salt and blend for a further
30 seconds.

Note: Store in an airtight container in the refrigerator for up to
4 weeks. The peanut butter will harden up in the refrigerator, but
will return to being more liquid at room temperature.

Almond butter

Fantastic in granola, or just spread on a cracker or an apple!

---

12 oz (340 g) raw, unsalted almonds
pinch of salt, or to taste

Preheat the oven to 350°F (180°C). Line a baking tray with baking paper.

Spread the almonds evenly over the baking tray. Roast in the preheated oven for 15 minutes, stirring once halfway through.

Allow the almonds to cool for 5 minutes. Process the almonds in a food processor for about 6 minutes, or until the almond butter is smooth and soft. Add salt and blend for a further 30 seconds.

Note: Store in an airtight container in the refrigerator for up to 4 weeks. The almond butter will harden up in the refrigerator, but will return to being more liquid at room temperature.

Caramel sauce

Designed to be the perfect consistency for my caramel granolas, this sweet sauce is
also fantastic eaten by the spoonful!

6¾ oz (190 g) white sugar
1 oz (30 g) butter or margarine
3 fl oz (90 ml) milk

Heat the sugar in a saucepan over medium–low heat. Stir often while the sugar starts to melt and clump. The sugar will slowly turn brown. Continue stirring and scraping down the sides until the sugar has all become liquid, and is an amber-brown color throughout. Be careful that the caramel does not burn.

Once the sugar is melted, quickly add the butter or margarine while still on the heat. The caramel will immediately begin to boil rapidly. Stir the mixture until the butter is fully incorporated.

Slowly add the milk, stirring. Once again, the caramel will bubble. Keep stirring, and allow the mixture to boil for about 1 minute before removing from the heat. Leave to cool.

Note: Store in an airtight container in the refrigerator for up to 2 weeks.

Dried fruit

Instead of buying dried fruit, buy fresh and dry it yourself in your oven!

Ripe but firm fruit of your choice—try cranberries, strawberries, apples, pears, or any other fruit you like. Avoid fruit that is under- or over-ripe.

Preheat the oven to as low a temperature as it will go (often about 200°F/100°C, or lower). Line a baking tray with baking paper.

Wash the fruit thoroughly, and peel if using a fruit that requires peeling, such as pineapple. If using small berries or fruits, such as cranberries, sour cherries, or blueberries, they can be left whole. Otherwise, slice the fruit thinly (about 1¼ inch/5 mm thick).

Spread the fruit out evenly over the baking tray. Fruit slices or berries may be touching, but not layered on top of one another.

Let the fruit dry in the oven. Drying times will vary between fruits, but will often be about 2-6 hours, depending on the size of the pieces. Check the fruit every hour, and more often once it begins to look dehydrated. Flip the fruit every 1–2 hours for more even drying. Leave to cool completely.

Note: Store in an airtight container in the refrigerator for up to 2 weeks.

Chocolate hazelnut spread

MAKES ¾ CUP

A healthier version of store-bought chocolate hazelnut spreads, this makes delicious granola!

5½ oz (155 g) hazelnuts
1 tablespoon oil
2½ oz (75 g) cup brown sugar
½ oz (15 g) cocoa powder
½ teaspoon vanilla
pinch of salt, or to taste

Preheat the oven to 375°F (190°C). Line a baking tray with baking paper.

Spread the hazelnuts evenly across the baking tray. Bake for 10–12 minutes. Allow to cool for 5–10 minutes, then rub with a clean towel to remove as much of the skins as possible.

Add the nuts into a food processor, and process for 3-5 minutes, until they form a paste. Add the remaining ingredients, and process until smooth.

Notes: Store in an airtight container in the refrigerator for up to 4 weeks. The hazelnut butter will harden up in the refrigerator, but will return to being more liquid at room temperature.

This recipe isn't as sweet as most store-bought spreads, so add extra sugar if you have a sweet tooth!

Index

Acknowledgements

This book would not have been possible without the support of so many people.

Thank you, first, to my husband, Quinn, who has taken on so many roles for me as I worked on this project. From carting around huge boxes of granola that I couldn't lift, to ingredient shopping when I got busy, to brainstorming me through writer's block- your loving support has made this book possible.

To my biggest fans, my parents, who uncomplainingly tasted dozens of batches of granola, and sometimes even bought the ingredients (thanks for smuggling me peanut butter all the way to Europe!). Also, to my sister, who taste-tested despite her dislike of granola- that's dedication!

To my lovely Bec, without whom this book would never have been more than an idea and a dream.

To Neil and Sandi Barber, who generously gave me the recipe that later became my trail mix granola mix, and who helped keep me excited through this whole endeavor!

To Gordana Trifunovic, James Mills-Hicks, Diane Ward, and all the other amazing and talented people at New Holland Publishing, who were generous enough to give me this opportunity, kind enough to guide me through the process, and incredible enough to turn my simple ideas into something I can be truly proud of.

To Heather Muse, my incredible photographer, whose creative and artistic vision made my recipes look beautiful.

Finally, thank you to all my friends and family who have offered their support, crazy flavor ideas, and granola-eating expertise!

About the author

Elise Barber is a passionate baker and granola enthusiast. Her love for granola grew out of a desire to eat healthy, delicious food that would fuel her work as an elementary school music teacher and an amateur triathlete. With the huge variety of taste preferences among friends and family, Elise is constantly creating new flavors to keep up with demand! Elise spends her summer holidays running a micro-bakery out of her home kitchen, where she bakes granola, and other tasty snacks. Elise lives with her husband Quinn in the wintery city of Edmonton, Canada, although she considers the German Black Forest her second home. She takes inspiration from many sources, such as the hearty winter fare of her Canadian hometown and the fresh fruit harvests of the German summers.

First published in 2016 by New Holland Publishers Pty Ltd
London • Sydney • Auckland

The Chandlery, Unit 704, 50 Westminster Bridge Road, London SE1 7QY, United Kingdom
1/66 Gibbes Street, Chatswood, NSW 2067, Australia
5/39 Woodside Avenue, Northcote, Auckland 0627, New Zealand

www.newhollandpublishers.com

ISBN 9781742578453

Managing Director: Fiona Shultz
Publisher: Diane Ward
Editor: Gordana Trifunovic
Photographer: Heather Muse
Production Director: James Mills-Hicks
Printer: Hang Tai Printing

10 9 8 7 6 5 4 3 2 1

Keep up with New Holland Publishers on Facebook
www.facebook.com/NewHollandPublishers